EMOTIONAL INTELLIGENCE

YOUR FOUNDATION FOR SUCCESS

HAYLEY HESSELN AND JANICE GAIR

EI ADVANTAGE

FriesenPress

Suite 300 - 990 Fort St
Victoria, BC, V8V 3K2
Canada

www.friesenpress.com

ISBN
978-1-5255-6925-8 (Hardcover)
978-1-5255-6926-5 (Paperback)
978-1-5255-6927-2 (eBook)

1. Business & Economics, Personal Success

Distributed to the trade by The Ingram Book Company

Table of Contents

INTRODUCTION

Have you ever wondered why some people are wildly successful, even when all indicators would have predicted otherwise? The reverse might also be true. Years after graduation, the class valedictorian may not have achieved much, in spite of her high IQ. Research into this phenomenon resulted in the notion of another kind of intelligence—emotional intelligence, or EI. Emotional intelligence can be described as our ability to govern our own emotions. Those with higher EI are fully aware of their own emotions, strengths, and weaknesses and are accepting of themselves. They are also appropriately expressive and able to build and maintain trusting relationships. In times of challenge as well as during the daily grind, they are skilled at managing their stress and making thoughtful decisions.

As it turns out, emotional intelligence (EI) is a better predictor of success than IQ, all things considered. Daniel Goleman explains that IQ is important to perform many jobs; you need the technical and academic skills to perform many tasks. For example, if you are a surgeon or a pipefitter, you need to know how to repair valves! However, both the surgeon and the pipefitter skilled at managing stress and looking at situations realistically, two aspects of EI, will likely perform better relative to their peers without such skills.

So, what can you do if your emotional skills are lacking? The good news is that EI can be enhanced: you can significantly strengthen your emotional skills through coaching and self-study. Regardless of whether you are a student or a professional looking to sharpen essential skills, you can adopt the practices suggested in this workbook to be your best self.

This workbook is organized into five sections related to EI composites: self-perception, self-expression, interpersonal, decision making, and stress management.[1] In each section, you'll find a description of behaviours associated with strengths and weaknesses, and information about how associated skills relate to the workplace

---

1   This workbook complements the MHS EQ-i 2.0 leadership and workplace assessments.

and life in general. Within each section, you'll learn more about the three subscales that make up each composite. Each subscale is accompanied by three exercises to help you improve.

SELF-PERCEPTION

Self-Awareness

Self-Regard

Self-Actualization

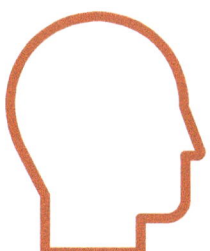

THE SELF

Daniel **Goleman** described self-awareness as "knowing one's internal states, preferences, resources and intuitions."[2] If we don't know ourselves, how are we supposed to better manage our emotions or use them to our greatest advantage? The idea of knowing ourselves is not new—it comes from the Ancient Greeks. You've likely heard the phrase, "know thyself," which has been expounded upon for centuries by philosophers. No wonder—it's an important part of our emotional intelligence.

Understanding ourselves is fundamental to emotional intelligence. It's important to be able to identify our feelings and why we are experiencing them. The modern, Western definition of "self-perception" encompasses our understanding of who we are and what we feel (self-awareness), our ability to feel confident and accept ourselves (self-regard), and our ability to pursue meaningful goals and continue to learn as we go through life (self-actualization).

Why is self-perception important, particularly from a business or leadership perspective? According to Peter Barron Stark, a company that has worked with thousands of leaders, an accurate self-perception is "absolutely critical" to success.[3] Many business gurus have stated the same, such as Peter Drucker in his book *Managing Oneself*.

> Success in the knowledge economy comes to those who know themselves, their strengths, their values, and how they best perform. We will be able to achieve results, remain competitive and be successful by knowing our strengths and limitations. Furthermore, by knowing

---

2   Goleman, D., 2015. How emotionally intelligent are you? Retrieved from: http://www.danielgoleman.info/daniel-goleman-how-emotionally-intelligent-are-you/

3   Peter Barron Stark., 2010. Leadership and Self Perceptions: How Do Others See You? Retrieved from: https://peterstark.com/leadership-and-self-perceptions/

our strengths and limitations, we can position ourselves where we can best contribute and excel within the organization.[4]

There has also been much research conducted on the relationship between self-perception and business success. Results overwhelmingly point to positive relationships that indicate stronger leadership, authentic behaviours, and stronger overall business results. [5,6,7,8]

4   UK Essays., 2013. Managing Oneself by Peter F. Trucker Management Essay. Retrieved from https://www.ukessays.com/essays/management/managing-oneself-by-peter-f-drucker-management-essay.php?vref=1

5   Luthans, F., Norman, S. & Hughes, L., 2006. *Authentic leadership. Inspiring leaders*, pp.84–104.

6   Noe, R., Hollenbeck, J., Gerhart, B., & Wright, P., 2006. *Human Resources Management: Gaining a Competitive Advantage,* Tenth Global Edition. McGraw-Hill Education.

7   Goleman, D., 2000. Leadership that gets results. *Harvard Business Review*, 78(2), pp.4–17.

8   Van Velsor, E., Taylor, S. & Leslie, J.B., 1993. An examination of the relationships among self-perception accuracy, self-awareness, gender, and leader effectiveness. *Human Resource Management*, 32(2–3), pp.249–263.

Self-Awareness

"Self-awareness gives you the capacity to learn from your mistakes as well as your successes. It enables you to keep growing." ~ Lawrence Bossidy[9]

Definition: Self-awareness is the capacity to recognize yourself: to understand your emotions and what causes them, and their effects. Being self-aware means that you can differentiate between subtleties in emotions and articulate the differences.

Highs—Highly self-aware people can accurately describe their emotions and understand the nuances between them. They are conscious of the effects their emotions have on themselves and others, and on their performance.

Lows—Those who are not very self-aware often don't know why they are experiencing certain thoughts and emotions. They might not be able to articulate emotional subtleties and might appear detached.

While self-awareness comes naturally to some, for those who are less self-aware, exercises can help to identify emotions, emotional triggers, and the consequences.

---

9   AZ Quotes.com,. No date. Retrieved from: https://www.azquotes.com/quote/830299

Exercise 1: Self-Awareness—Pull the trigger

We react to situations: our emotions are triggered by events. We also know them as buttons. Someone pushes our buttons, and we get angry. The first step to gaining more self-awareness is to identify your triggers. Read the following list of triggers and describe the emotions associated with each.

- Someone tried to control you.
- Someone tried to smother you.
- Someone was needy.
- You felt helpless.
- You received a disapproving look.
- You were blamed.
- You were criticized.
- You were ignored
- You were judged.
- You were overlooked for promotion.
- You were rejected.
- You were reprimanded.
- You were shamed.

Next, consider how you reacted to the triggers. Did you do the following:

- comply,
- get angry,
- blame others,
- use a vice (food, drugs, alcohol, etc.), or
- shut down emotionally?

What do you need to change to manage your emotions? Recognizing and preparing for your triggers can help you deal with situations before they occur.

Exercise 2: Self-Awareness—The Feeling Wheel

We *feel* emotions, but sometimes it's difficult to *articulate* or *label* what we are feeling. In some cases, we might not know fully what we are feeling.

Identifying an emotion can help us deal with it and act appropriately. For example, you will respond in one way if you are feeling contempt and another if you are feeling aggressive. Both emotions are related to *anger*.

Use the Plutchik Wheel to identify and articulate your emotions.

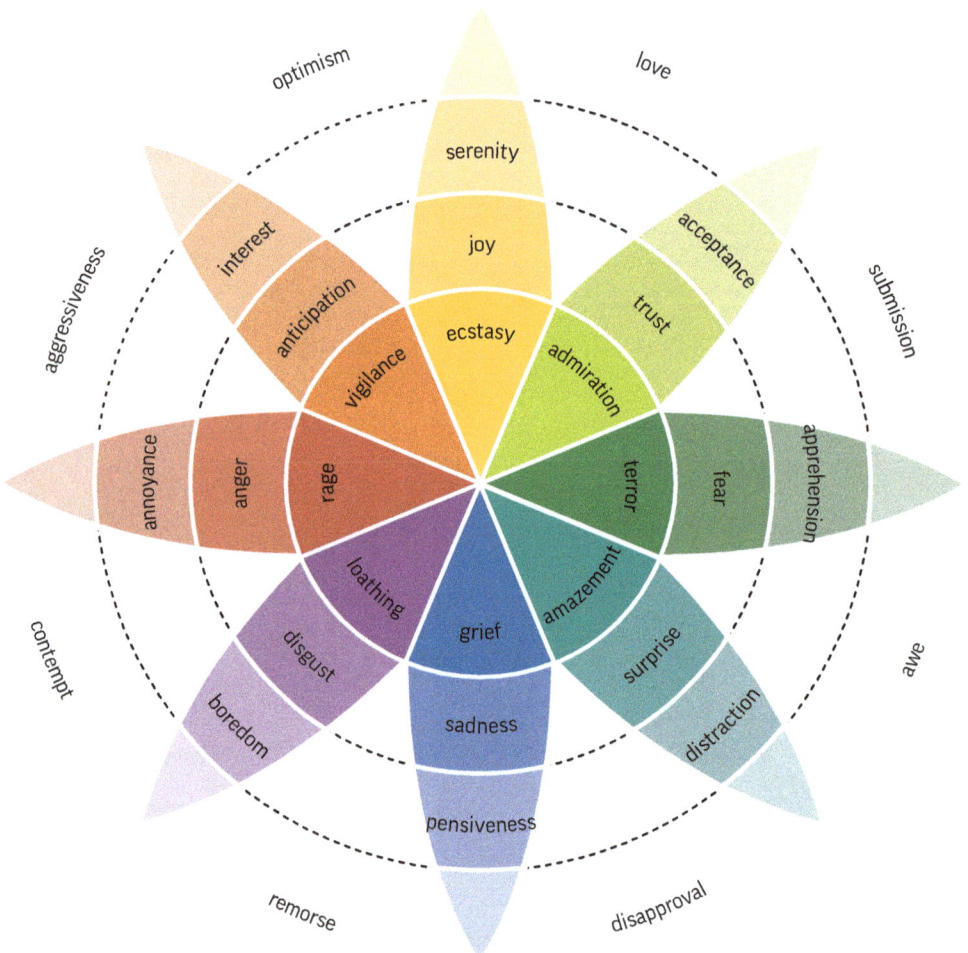

Plutchik Wheel of Emotion

Exercise 3: Self-Awareness—Emotional Tracking

You might consider documenting what is happening in your daily life by tracking your emotional responses to different situations. Do this for two weeks, taking note of how you react to different events and different people in different settings.

Reflect on what you discover and watch for patterns at home and work. What did you learn? Were some types of emotions more prevalent than others? For example, did you feel emotions that were more positive (love, happiness) or negative (anger, fear)?

What will you change, if anything?

Self-Regard

"What lies behind us and what lies before us are tiny matters compared to what lies within us." ~ Ralph Waldo Emerson[10]

Definition: Self-regard, also related to self-esteem, is our ability to have consideration for ourselves, including recognizing and accepting our strengths and weaknesses. Self-regard also affects our confidence.

Highs—Individuals that demonstrate high self-regard tend to be confident and self-assured. They understand and accept their own strengths and weaknesses. Those with very high self-regard can appropriately manage it and not come across as arrogant.

Lows—Those who have little self-regard are often withdrawn and lack confidence. They over-emphasize their weaknesses and dwell on their faults. While humility can be beneficial, it's important to recognize our strengths and accept ourselves.

---

10 Pass it on., No date. Retrieved from: https://www.passiton.com/
inspirational-quotes/3392-what-lies-behind-us-and-what-lies-before-us

Exercise 1: Self-Regard—Rewrite Your Story

Does that little voice in your head hold you back? Does it keep telling you that you'll fail, that you don't have what it takes? That's known as self-talk, and if you tell yourself something often enough, you will start to believe it. Dr. Jennice Vilhauer suggests that you can change the self-talk to focus on the positive.[11]

1. Notice the critic—Take note each time you have a critical thought about yourself. What are the patterns that emerge? What are the words you most frequently hear?
2. Free yourself—Name your critic and start to recognize that it isn't you talking. It's the negative voice.
3. Dispute the message—Rather than having a negative thought and letting it negatively affect you, replace the message. If the voice is telling you that you can't do something, refute that and think, "I can do what I put my mind to."
4. Replace the message—Learn to reframe the negative messages using positive language. If you tend to think, "I can't," or "I won't," start to say "I can" and "I will." Take note of how you feel. Make it a habit.

---

11 Vilhauer, J., 2016. 4 Ways to Stop Beating Yourself Up, Once and For All. Retrieved from: https://www.psychologytoday.com/ca/blog/living-forward/201603/4-ways-stop-beating-yourself-once-and-all

Exercise 2: Self-Regard—Don't Compare and Despair

A great article by Ali Binns, a behavioural therapist in the UK, describes the condition known as *compare and despair*.[12] It's highly prevalent and can be very destructive, leading to anxiety, a lack of self-worth, and depression—all of which can destroy confidence. She recommends that you start to employ these three steps to overcoming this destructive form of thought.

1. Balance—Reframe your thoughts about yourself. Learn to accept compliments and focus on what you do well.
2. Let go of obstructive thoughts—Stop making excuses for compliments. Let go of negative thoughts and mindfully replace them with positive facts.
3. Build self-compassion—Nobody is perfect, and that's OK. Start to forgive yourself and let go of the burdens you have been carrying.

Consider how you will accomplish this. Document what will you commit to.

---

12 Binns, A., 2018. Unhelpful thinking styles: compare and despair. Retrieved from: http://www. alibinns.co.uk/resources/unhelpful-thinking-styles-compare-and-despair

Exercise 3: Self-Regard—Improve Your Confidence

If you aren't that confident, all is not lost. It's possible to build confidence, but it takes practice and effort, and it won't happen overnight. A website dedicated to developing essential skills suggests three steps to take.[13]

1. Prepare yourself. Take stock of your strengths, weaknesses, threats, and opportunities, and be mindful about where you're going. What do you want out of life? Having goals can help you identify what is important and, therefore, better guide you forward. Once you have a sense of yourself in the present, you must commit to change.

   Strengths

   Weaknesses

   Threats

   Opportunities

2. Get started. Embarking on your journey requires information and a change in habits. Start by identifying the skills you will need, and then find ways to build these skills. You should also start with small wins and set goals you can achieve to help you get into the habit of achieving them. During this time, it's important to ensure that your negative self-talk doesn't take over. Be positive, focus on what you have accomplished.

   My skills

3. Keep going. Your positive practice should be giving you the confidence to set higher and more difficult goals. Reach further and stretch yourself. Be sure to continue to set goals.

   My goals

---

13 Mind Tools., No date. Building self-confidence. Retrieved from: https://www.mindtools.com/selfconf.html

Self-Actualization

"Only those who attempt the absurd will achieve the impossible." ~ Albert Einstein[14]

Definition: Self-actualization is the willingness and drive for meaning and life-long learning. Self-actualization is also about the pursuit of objectives that matter and will allow you to lead a rich and enjoyable life.

Highs—Highly self-actualized people tend to be enthusiastic in their pursuit of goals, act with great purpose, and are self-motivated. They seek opportunities to learn.

Lows—Less self-actualized individuals set fewer goals and are not motivated to seek growth or opportunities to learn. They might not make full use of their strengths, and they might focus on insignificant tasks rather than the big picture.

Research shows that self-actualization is critical to leadership and overall happiness.[15]

---

14 Pass it on., No date. Retried from: https://www.passiton.com/inspirational-quotes/7059-only-those-who-attempt-the-absurd-can-achieve

15 Stein, S.J. & Book, H.E., 2011. *The EQ Edge: Emotional intelligence and your success*. John Wiley & Sons.

Exercise 1: Self-Actualization—Values

Self-actualization is all about living with meaning and having goals that matter to you—something you can strive for and that has value. What are *your* values? Do an Internet search for "core values" to see what comes up.

Next, take some time to reflect on your own values.

1. Select your top three to five values.
2. Give examples of why they matter to you.
3. Think about how your decisions are aligned (or not) with your values.
4. Consider whether your career goals and life choices are fulfilling your values.
5. If they are, great! If not, what might you need to do differently to help you find meaning in your actions?

Exercise 2: Self-Actualization—Goal Setting

If we have nothing to plan or strive for, life can be meaningless. It's important to find meaning so that you can pursue goals with purpose and feel a sense of accomplishment and satisfaction. Kanoy and others suggest you consider both personal and professional goals.[16]

My professional goals	My personal goals
I receive the most enjoyment from (e.g. friends, volunteering, working, studying, family, etc.)	I receive the most meaning from (e.g. volunteering, collaborating, being with my family, etc.)

1. Who has helped you shape your goals?
2. What experiences in your life thus far have mattered the most? Why?
3. What is your most important goal?
   - When will you start to work toward it?
   - Who can/will help you?
   - When do you expect to achieve your goal?
   - How will you feel when you get there?

---

16 Kanoy, K., Book, H.E., & Stein, S.J., 2013. *The Student EQ Edge: Emotional Intelligence and Your Academic and Personal Success: Student Workbook*. John Wiley and Sons: San Francisco.

Exercise 3: Self-Actualization— The Pursuit of Growth

Scott Jeffrey explains the power of Maslow's findings on self-actualization and provides advice on how to become more motivated.[17] This resource provides five steps to begin the process.

1. Identify your core strengths.
2. Stay centred and focused.
3. Articulate your personal vision.
4. Develop a personal development plan.
5. Be mindful of and overcome resistance.

---

17 Jeffrey, S., No date. A Complete Guide to Self-Actualization: 5 Key Steps to Accelerate Growth. Retrieved from: https://scottjeffrey.com/self-actualization/

SELF EXPRESSION

Self-expression

Assertiveness

Independence

EXPRESSION

Dale Carnegie said that "self-expression is the dominant necessity of human nature."[18] To develop relationships and communicate, we need to express ourselves. While we mostly communicate through talking, our intentions and emotions are expressed through our language, our specific word choice, tone, and intonation. In addition to speaking, we also communicate with body language. Think of what crossed arms, rolling eyes, or the lack of eye contact might tell you. It's remarkable how much information can be conveyed without the use of a single word.

The self-expression composite is made up of three aspects of how we express ourselves: emotional expression, assertiveness, and independence. People skilled in self-expression can convey their thoughts and feelings using a full range of emotions; they do so in a way that is assertive yet not aggressive nor damaging to relationships, and they stand by their core values and beliefs. Individuals lacking in this regard tend not to express emotions at all, or are unbalanced in expressing more positive or negative emotions. They also might display passive-aggressive behaviour and not take into consideration how their own expression of ideas negatively affects others. Finally, individuals having difficulty with emotional expression might be somewhat dependent—they might not be able to stand by their ideas, take responsibility for their beliefs, or express their thoughts when those thoughts are not aligned with the majority view.

Expression is important in the workplace for a variety of reasons. Consider a person you know who does not express what they are thinking. Their lack of expression likely makes it difficult for you to gauge their mood, thoughts, beliefs, and ultimately, to communicate. Research also supports the importance of self-expression in the workplace and for leadership. A study by Ilies and others indicates that more

---

18 Relicsworld,. No date. Retrieved from: https://www.relicsworld.com/dale-carnegie/
self-expression-is-the-dominant-necessity-of-human-nature-author

expressive leaders tend to have highly-motivated followers, and that those leaders are perceived to be more effective.[19] Additionally, emotionally-expressive leaders are seen to be more visionary.[20]

19 Ilies R., Curşeu P.L., Dimotakis N., & Spitzmuller M., 2013. Leaders' emotional expressiveness and their behavioural and relational authenticity: Effects on followers. *European Journal of Work and Organizational Psychology*. Feb 1;22(1):4–14.

20 Groves K.S., 2006. Leader emotional expressivity, visionary leadership, and organizational change. *Leadership & Organization Development Journal*. Oct 1;27(7):566-83.

Emotional Expression

"We try to hide our feelings, but we forgot that our eyes speak." ~ Unknown[21]

Definition: Emotional expression refers to the full way in which we express ourselves. It includes the language we use, our tone of voice, facial expressions, our body language, and even silence.

Highs—Highly expressive people can comfortably express a wide range of emotions; they have an expansive emotional vocabulary and recognize the importance of being expressive.

Lows—Less expressive people might find communication awkward and uncomfortable, might appear withdrawn and quiet, are typically uneasy with emotional situations, and have a limited emotional vocabulary.

---

21 Brain Quotes., No date. Retrieved from: http://www.braintrainingtools.org/skills/
try-to-hide-our-feelings/

Exercise 1: Emotional Expression— Understanding

Susan Krauss-Whitbourne connects emotional self-perception with expression. To express ourselves, we need to know what we are feeling and why.[22] She recommends four ways to improve emotional communication.

1. Perceive emotions—Recognize what you are feeling and what caused those feelings.
2. Facilitate emotion—Evaluate the emotions you are feeling and use them to manage your behaviour in each situation.
3. Understand emotion—Know where your emotions come from and predict what you might feel in response to different situations.
4. Manage emotion—Stay the course. Rather than flying into a rage when you hear bad news, expect what the news might be, and be prepared to be calm and to use emotions that will support the situation rather than make it worse.

To practise this exercise, consider a situation in which you were unable to express emotions, or in which you expressed emotions inappropriately, causing a difficult situation to escalate.

1. Describe the situation and the emotions you were feeling and why.
2. Review how you facilitated your emotions. What language did you use? Were you aware of your facial features? What did your body language express?
3. Did you expect to feel this way? Did you prepare for this event/situation?
4. How will you prepare in the future? How could you have expressed yourself differently? What might have been the outcome?

---

22 Krauss-Whitbourne, S., 2014. 4 Ways to improve your emotional communication. Retrieved from: https://www.psychologytoday.com/us/blog/fulfillment-any-age/201412/4-ways-improve-your-emotional-communication

Exercise 2: Emotional Expression— How to Approach It

Part of the difficulty in expressing emotion can be the words we use. We might say something that is perceived as blame when it wasn't intended that way. We also must be careful not to express emotions (something we feel) as thoughts. Susan Heitler provides some guidance for how to express feelings, and more importantly, how *not* to express feelings.[23]

What to avoid:

"I feel …" versus "I feel that …" The first expression is the way to go if you are expressing feelings. If you are expressing thoughts, go with the second phrase. She highlights some problems with how we use language.

"You make me feel …" should be avoided for a variety of reasons:

- It might sound accusatory.
- It can be disempowering.
- It invites counter-accusations.
- It could cause a misunderstanding about what triggers feelings.
- It misplaces focus on the other person rather than yourself.

Good practices:

1. Take time to identify your feelings.
2. Be careful about anger and being defensive. If you feel this way, wait until the intensity passes.
3. To promote your ability to be heard, replace intense words with less intense words from the same family (see the Plutchik Wheel in "Self-Perception").
4. Start your discussion with "I feel …" or a variation depending on tense ("I felt …").
5. Explain why you feel the way you do.
6. Explain your speaking partner's role objectively without blame (e.g. "You did this…" or "I felt that …").

---

23 Heitler, S., 2013. How to express feelings… and how not to. Retrieved from: https://www.psychologytoday.com/ca/blog/resolution-not-conflict/201305/how-express-feelings-and-how-not

Review these practices using a situation in which you had difficulty expressing your feelings. Go through each step and review your feelings, the words you used, and the consequences of the discussion. This could also be done with a conversation you witnessed that was emotionally charged.

Exercise 3: Emotional Expression—
What's your style?

We all communicate differently and express our emotions to different degrees and in a range of ways. Being expressive also means we have to respond to how others are expressing themselves. Astrid Baumgardner discusses four communication styles: driver, analytical, expressive, and amiable.[24] She also explains how best to express ourselves with others.

- Drivers take charge and seek solutions. To communicate with drivers, it's best to stay focused and on point, be decisive, and offer relevant points.
- Analytical communicators tend to want details. To better communicate, it's useful to be prepared with facts and data, to be thorough and rational.
- Expressive individuals are about ideas. Communication with someone expressive should focus on the big picture, vision, and ideals.
- Amiable people put relationships first. Communication in this category would best be served by an approach that is warm and friendly and focuses on the relationships among people involved.

To best leverage these skills, consider the following questions:

- What type of communicator do you tend to be?
- What skills would be valuable for you to strengthen?
- What types of emotions do you feel when communicating with people who use different styles?
- How do you regulate emotions when conversing with other types of communicators?
- What might you need to do to adapt to situations in which you feel uncomfortable?

---

24 Baumgardner, A., 2011. Power up your communication: how to leverage the 4 communication styles. Retrieved from: https://www.astridbaumgardner.com/blog-and-resources/articles/communication-styles/

Assertiveness

"Nobody can make you feel inferior without your consent." ~ Eleanor Roosevelt[25]

Definition: Being assertive is the ability to communicate your thoughts, opinions, beliefs, and values openly and in a way that is socially acceptable and does not damage interpersonal relations. Being assertive also means standing up for your beliefs when you are not in the majority, and being responsible for your actions.

Highs—Assertive individuals can express their thoughts and feelings without being aggressive and offensive; they are firm in their beliefs and will stand by their opinions. They stand up for themselves and others and use emotions objectively to do so. Assertive individuals are also aware that assertiveness can appear as aggression, so they moderate their own behaviour.

Lows—Less assertive Individuals might appear quiet and are unlikely to stand up for themselves or others; they rarely express their views, particularly when such views are controversial or unpopular. Such individuals might also seem passive, or even passive-aggressive.

Assertiveness is an important element of emotional intelligence and can affect our happiness. Research shows that individuals who report success in life tend to be assertive.[26]

---

25 Quote Investigator., 2012. No One Can Make You Feel Inferior Without Your Consent. Retrieved from: https://quoteinvestigator.com/2012/04/30/no-one-inferior/

26 Stein, S.J. & Book, H.E., 2011. *The EQ Edge: Emotional Intelligence and Your Success*. John Wiley & Sons.

Exercise 1: Assertiveness—Start Small

If you are not an assertive person, you can take steps to gradually feel comfortable with expressing yourself clearly and without fear. Blaz Kos has some great tips for becoming more assertive, some of which are listed here. For a full review of steps to assertiveness, visit his blog.[27]

Three steps from the blog recommend that you:

1. Develop awareness of your emotions—What are your needs? You could make a list and connect emotions to those needs.
2. Reflect on your own behaviour—When are you assertive, aggressive, passive-aggressive, or passive? What are the characteristics of each situation? Is there a pattern?
3. Face your fears and, with the examples above, start to practise being more assertive. Start small and move to more uncomfortable situations as you gain experience.

Be sure to practise.

Take note of what has changed. Reflect on the changes in your emotions when being assertive.

---

27 Koz, B., No date. How to become more assertive with a few simple exercises. https://agileleanlife. com/how-to-become-more-assertive/

Exercise 2: Assertiveness—Speak up!

People who are not assertive generally try to avoid confrontation and conflict; therefore, they don't speak up when they need to. However, not speaking up over time can start to damage self-regard and ultimately leave you feeling helpless. Start small and have an arsenal of objective language to use. Meg Selig suggests trying prepared phrases.[28]

- "Thanks, but I'm not interested."
- "Thanks, but I can't make that a priority right now."
- "Thanks, but I need some time to myself right now."
- "Thanks, but no thanks."
- "No thanks."
- "Thanks for thinking of me, but I'll pass on this one."
- "Thanks for keeping me in the loop, but I can't make it this time."
- "Thank you for sharing, but I'd like to hear from other people in the group."
- "I appreciate that you enjoy doing _____, but it's really not my scene."
- "I'll think about it and get back to you."
- "I just don't know. Mind if I think about it for a while?"
- "This is so important, and I can't give it the time it deserves right now. Can we make an appointment to talk?"
- "I didn't appreciate _____ (what you did, your tone of voice)."
- "I appreciated _____."
- "I disagree with you. I see the situation this way."
- "I would like you to respect my point of view."
- "I feel offended by your remark."
- "My policy is _____ (e.g. not to date people at work)." Note that it's hard to argue with a policy statement. It's your policy!

Develop phrases that feel right for you.

For more advice and information on assertiveness, see the blog *The Assertiveness Habit*, by the same author.[29]

---

28 Selig, M., 2012. Speak Up! 18 all-purpose assertive phrases. Retrieved from: https://www. psychologytoday.com/ca/blog/changepower/201210/speak-18-all-purpose-assertive-phrases

29 Selig, M., 2012. The assertiveness habit. Retrieved from: https:// www.psychologytoday.com/ca/ blog/changepower/201209/the-assertiveness-habit

Exercise 3: Assertiveness—Quit Being a Pushover

The advice on the website, *The Art of Manliness*, does not pertain just to men.[30] Brett and Kate McKay provide a great summary discussion on the benefits of being assertive, which include improved relationships, greater confidence, lower stress, and less resentment. Being able to say what we mean, and to stand up for ourselves is empowering! To be passive, to be a pushover, and to be unable to say "no" can be draining and demoralizing.

The only way to become assertive is to do it: practise and make it a habit. How do you get started?

1. Change your mindset—You need to think differently and want to change. Recommendations include:
   - Set boundaries—Make a list of the rules you will live by, such as not checking work email after hours. What is non-negotiable?
   - Take responsibility—Take control of what you need to change and don't blame others.
   - Speak up—Nobody can read your mind. What are you prepared to say?
   - Release control—You are not responsible for how others respond to you. If you have been passive in your life, you might get resistance and pushback. That's OK. Keep going.
   - Be civil—Being assertive is about expressing yourself in a non-damaging, objective manner. No need to be aggressive.
   - Be patient—Things don't change overnight. Recognize that changing behaviour and developing new habits takes time and that you will likely not be successful 100% of the time.

2. Practise—While it's nice to think about making changes, you can only improve by acting more assertively.
   - Start with small contributions to conversations that are relatively low risk.
   - Learn to say no, and practise with phrases that feel comfortable.
   - Be simple, direct, and objective. It's OK to say "no thanks" without a litany of excuses.

---

30 McKay, B. K., & McKay, K., 2018. Quit being a pushover: how to be assertive. Retrieved from: https://www.artofmanliness.com/articles/how-to-be-assertive/

- Change your language. Rather than blaming or pointing fingers, use "I" statements, such as "I feel...".
- Don't apologize for reasonable requests when you are practising directives.
- Adjust your body language and vocabulary to build confidence.
- Pick your battles. It is not necessary to always be assertive, especially over things that you don't much care about.
- Practise and be persistent. Don't give up—you will get there in time.

Independence

"To find yourself, think for yourself." ~ Socrates (Classic Greek philosopher)[31]

Definition: Being independent is about standing on our own two feet—taking responsibility for our actions, making self-directed choices, and not being emotionally reliant on others. While it is definitely good to consider others' opinions and feelings, being independent means that after we've gathered the data, we're able to make decisions and remain accountable.

Highs—Highly independent individuals can make decisions independent from others, solve problems, and work in a self-directed manner without the need for support. They are directive and decisive.

Lows—People who tend toward dependency are often emotionally reliant on others for support, are not willing to take responsibility for their actions, and tend to be followers. They often need reassurance and prefer activities and jobs that are well defined with clear direction.

Being emotionally independent is essential for strong leadership. Decision making, particularly where emotions are concerned, requires individuals to be secure enough with themselves to take responsibility for outcomes.

---

31 Quotes., No date. Retrieved from: https://www.quotes.net/quote/38684

Exercise 1: Independence—Think Like a Leader

"It takes courage to have your own thoughts," according to Avery Blank at Forbes.[32] Independent people can process information and stand alone in their thoughts without succumbing to *groupthink*. It is not easy to stand alone, but you can improve your ability to think independently by doing the following:

- Read more—Consider other perspectives and views, expand your horizons, and seek to challenge your ideas.
- See different perspectives—Challenge your own views by playing Devil's advocate.
- Seek diversity—Interact with people who hold different views and opinions. You might find you become less rooted in your own thinking.
- Travel—Pursue experiences in different countries and cultures to expand your world.
- Focus on respect—While you might stand alone with your ideas, you can be respectful of others.

Explain how you will commit to becoming more independent:

---

32 Blank, A., 2018. 5 Ways to become an independent thinker and show your leadership. Forbes, July 24, 2018. Retrieved from: https://www.forbes.com/sites/averyblank/2018/07/24/5-ways-to-become-an-independent-thinker-and-show-your-leadership/#4c96de0d24a1

Exercise 2: Independence—Take Responsibility

Being independent means that you not only have your own thoughts and ideas, but you are willing to stand up for your actions and be accountable. There are steps you can take that build on emotional skills reviewed in "Self-Perception" to help develop your independence, including being emotionally self-aware and taking initiative.

1. What do you need to act independently? Make a list of information or skills required to take the initiative.
2. What is stopping you from acting? Identify the emotions you experience when you consider acting independently.
3. What will it take for you to take initiative?
4. How will you take ownership of successes and failures without making excuses?
5. How will you get over negative emotions associated with being independent?

Exercise 3: Independence—Empower Others

Mac McIntire provides sage advice regarding how to help others become independent through empowerment.[33] While it's nice to be independent, sometimes acting alone in a business is not the best practice. There are levels of responsibility, and actions that often require approval. The model below can be used to help define tasks that can help you and others to act independently.

There are three zones: black, green, and red, which vary by task. There are also two conditions: responsibility and accountability.

BLACK ZONE
Sum of all tasks

RED ZONE
Tasks for which
employee
needs approval

GREEN ZONE
Tasks for which
employee
has authority

BLACK ZONE
Employee
Responsible

RED ZONE
Shared
Accountability

GREEN ZONE
Employee
Accountable

Responsibility: the tasks for which you must perform.

Accountability: tasks for which you are answerable regarding outcomes.

Green Zone: List the tasks for which you have full authority and are, therefore, fully accountable.

Red Zone: Tasks in this area require approval. This means that you and someone else (your supervisor, perhaps) share accountability. Make a list of the tasks in this area that require approval and the persons responsible for that approval.

Black Zone: This area includes both tasks that fall under shared responsibility and full accountability. Make a list of tasks and document the individuals (including yourself) who are responsible and accountable.

---

33 McIntire, M., 2011. How to empower employees to make effective decisions on the front-line. Innovation Management Group, Las Vegas, NV. Retrieved from: http://www.imglv.com/articles/how_to_empower_employees.pdf

INTERPERSONAL

Interpersonal

Empathy

Social Responsibility

RELATIONSHIPS

The interpersonal realm reflects how well you interact with others. This means developing and maintaining meaningful relationships and managing them using empathy and care for the greater good. People skilled in this realm are authentic, open, and trusting. They can manage their own emotions to better connect with others. They can read people and know when to adjust their own behaviour.

Interpersonal relations are highly important in the workplace because regardless of where you work, you will have to connect with others, such as your superiors, colleagues, peers, direct reports, and customers. We cannot get through life without relating to others. Research demonstrates that individuals skilled in this realm encourage a greater degree of engagement with employees, which leads to more positive relationships, greater productivity, and healthier working environments.[34] Social responsibility is also highly important, particularly when combined with corporate goals to give back to communities. As leaders, it's important to consider the greater good.

Empathy, a critical part of the interpersonal realm, is equal to none when it comes to social effectiveness, according to Daniel Goleman and others.[35] Transformative leaders score higher in empathy, can understand and relate to others' emotions, are sensitive to others' feelings, and can adjust their own behaviour accordingly.[36] While you might not be born with empathy, it's something that can be learned. The following exercises are designed to help you improve emotions associated with the interpersonal realm.

34 Hansen, A., Byrne, Z., & Kiersch, C., 2014. How interpersonal leadership relates to employee engagement. *Journal of Managerial Psychology*, Vol. 29 Issue: 8, pp.953-972, *https://doi.org/10.1108/JMP-11-2012-0343*

35 Goleman, D., Boyatzis, R., & McKee, A., 2002. The emotional reality of teams. *Journal of Organizational Excellence*, 21(2), pp.55-65.

36 Mathew, M., & Gupta, K.S,. 2015. Transformational leadership: Emotional intelligence. *SCMS Journal of Indian Management*, 12(2), 75-89.

Interpersonal Relations

"No one cares how much you know, until they know how much you care."
~ Theodore Roosevelt[37]

Definition: This subscale reflects a person's ability to develop and maintain meaningful relationships that are built on trust, openness, compassion, and understanding of others' emotions, both individually and as a social group. People skilled in this area are authentic and care about the greater good.

Highs—Those skilled in interpersonal relations can use emotional information and modify their behaviour accordingly. They are able to establish strong relationships and networks, can rely on others, and are genuinely sociable and caring.

Lows—Individuals less skilled in this area can be defensive and closed to others. They are not able to build networks or rely on others, and often do not trust others. They are not able to build bonds where give and take are mutually recognized.

The subscales in the interpersonal realm are highly interrelated. To develop and maintain meaningful and mutually satisfying relationships, we must be authentic and trusting; we need to be empathic and consider the greater good. Some of the exercises for this realm help to build relationships in several ways.

---

37 Brainy Quote., No date. Retrieved from: https://www.brainyquote.com/quotes/ theodore_roosevelt_140484

Exercise 1: Interpersonal—Be Curious

Have you ever noticed that people really like to talk? And more importantly, they like to talk about themselves? Take advantage of this to help build relationships. Rather than talking about yourself, start to ask questions that help you get to know others. Be curious. Be open. Enjoy your conversation. It also helps in awkward social situations when you feel you don't have much to say. A great way to approach this type of conversation is something known as "appreciative inquiry," as reflected by the question types below.[38]

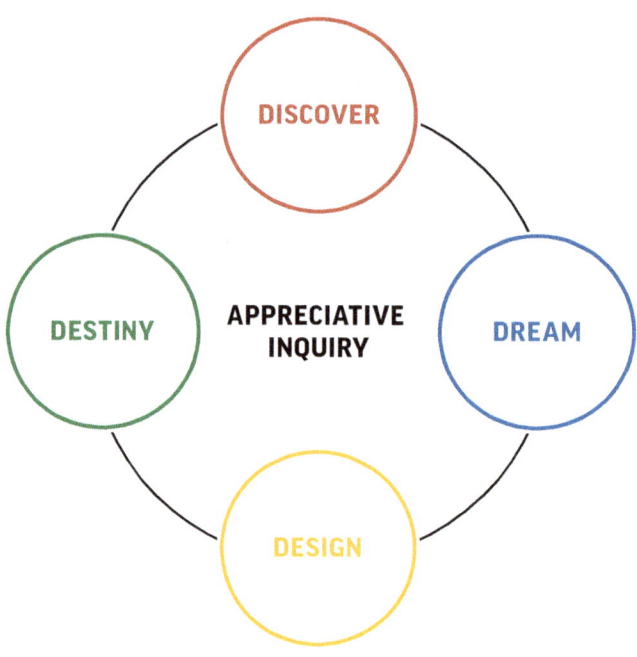

Discovery—"What brings you to this event?"

Dream—"What do you hope to get out of this event?"

Design—"How could we work together in the future?"

Destiny—"What's the most valuable aspect of your work?"

---

38 Cooperrider, D.L. & Srivastva, S., 1987. Appreciative inquiry in organizational life. *Research in Organizational Change and Development*, 1(1), pp.129–169.

Example: You're at a networking event and at a loss for words. Generate a list of questions that you could use to break the ice and possibly develop a greater understanding of someone.

Design your own questions around the four Ds:

Exercise 2: Interpersonal—Trust Building

Randy Conley proposes to lead with trust.[39] Trust is a significant and important aspect of relationships, whether they are highly personal or more business-oriented. If your direct reports don't trust you, they're less likely to engage or put themselves out. If your customers don't trust you, they'll shop elsewhere. If your boss doesn't trust you, you might not have a job for long. Answer the following questions and determine how you could increase your trustworthiness in the future.

- How do you follow through on your commitments?
- How do you demonstrate an interest in others?
- To what extent do you tell the truth?
- Have you been known to gossip?
- Are you known to keep confidences?
- To what degree do you incorporate others' ideas?
- How often do you praise people for their efforts?
- Could you be more responsive to requests?
- How will you ensure that you under-promise and over-deliver?
- How will you build a stronger rapport with others?

---

39 Conley, R., No date. Leading with trust. *Leadingwithtrust.com*. Retrieved at: https://leadingwith-trust.com/2018/09/16/25-ways-to-immediately-build-trust-at-work/

Exercise 3: Interpersonal—Authenticity

Authenticity is about being real and genuine, open and trustworthy. Strong leaders demonstrate authenticity by acting as a role model and treating people fairly. As a result, they are often seen as ethical and worthy of high regard. The Forbes Coaches Council offers sound advice when it comes to being authentic.[40]

1. Articulate your purpose—What do you need to accomplish?
2. Review your values—Do they include being genuine, truthful, focused, and determined?
3. Strengthen your discipline—How can you lead by example?
4. Demonstrate your passion—Are you leading with your heart?

---

40 Forbes Coaches Council., 2017. What it really takes to be an authentic leader. *Forbes. com*. May 11, 2017. https://www.forbes.com/sites/forbescoachescouncil/2017/05/11/what-it-really-takes-to-be-an-authentic-leader/#1db0c9475d09

Empathy

"Empathy is seeing with the eyes of another, listening with the ears of another, and feeling with the heart of another." ~ Alfred Adler[41]

Definition: The formal definition of empathy is the ability to understand and share the feelings of another, to be able to see things from another's perspective, and to show concern.

Highs—Those high in empathy are aware of and can appreciate others' feelings; they can "read" people and consider their own actions according to how others feel.

Lows—People who are not empathic struggle to understand how people feel, and they don't recognize how their own behaviours affect others. They are often insensitive to others' needs and might misinterpret or misread the feelings of individuals or groups.

Empathy is an important part of life. Being able to recognize how people feel and acting on it will greatly enhance your interpersonal skills and your ability to be a team player. Empathy should not be confused with sympathy—it's not the case that you need to feel the same way, to sympathize, to feel pity, or to feel sorry for another's misfortunes. Empathy is about recognition, understanding, and acknowledging.

---

41 Goodreads., No date. Retrieved from: https://www.goodreads.com/quotes/776552-seeing-with-the-eyes-of-another-listening-with-the-ears

Exercise 1: Empathy—Get Perspective

Have you ever been in a situation where you really didn't get where the person was coming from? You just didn't see it their way or couldn't put yourself in their shoes? Perhaps there was a time when you knew for a fact they were wrong.

Take a look at the image of the two people arguing. Who is correct?

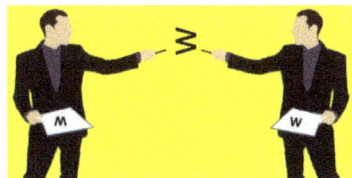

They *both* are. It's often helpful to take a step back and consider whether we are seeing things from all perspectives. It's difficult to do because we tend to be set in our ways. Here are some steps that can help you see things from a different perspective.[42]

1. Assess your assumptions
   - What are your beliefs?
   - What are your expectations?
   - What are the facts?

2. Expand your thinking.
   - What is possible?
   - What has worked before?
   - What have you not tried?

3. Get perspective.
   - What would you do?
   - What do you see?
   - What would others do?

Use the questions above to help guide you through a situation where you're stuck, or where you don't quite see eye to eye. Describe the situation and write down the answers to each of the questions. When you're done, reflect on what you discovered.

42 Heshmat, S., 2015. The wisdom behind the saying, "get some perspective." *Psychology Today*. April 6, 2015. Retrieved from: https://www.psychologytoday.com/ca/blog/science-choice/201504/the-wisdom-behind-the-saying-get-some-perspective

Exercise 2: Empathy—Active Listening

Are you a good listener? Most people think they are, but they really aren't. We tend to think about what we're going to say next during a conversation and focus on our own contributions rather than really listening. When you are listening deeply, you are not distracted, and your full attention is on the person with whom you are communicating. That means you're listening to what they say, how they say it, the emotions involved, and the body language.

Before you begin this exercise, observe people around you in conversations. What do you notice? Are people really listening to each other? Explain what you see.

Dianne Schilling at *Forbes* magazine has great suggestions to be a better listener.[43] During your next conversation, practise the following:

- Face the speaker and maintain eye contact (but don't be weird).
- Relax, but be attentive.
- Be open-minded about what the speaker is saying (and don't jump in).
- Try to understand what the individual is saying. Put yourself in their shoes.
- Don't interrupt. Use natural pauses to let the speaker finish their thoughts and express themselves fully.
- Ask for clarification to ensure you're on track. This is a good place to use appreciative inquiry to learn better the meaning of what's being said without coming up with your own solutions.
- Try to change your perspective by understanding what the speaker feels.
- Give regular feedback based on what you hear.
- Listen to what the speaker is not saying. What is their body language telling you?

Reflect on the exercise. Was the exercise easy or difficult? Explain why.

- What did you learn about yourself and about the speaker?
- Did you notice any difference in how the speaker responded to you when you were actively listening?
- What was different about this experience compared to other conversations?

---

43 Schilling, D., 2012. 10 steps to effective listening. *Forbes Women.*
    November 9, 2012. Retrieved from: https://www.forbes.com/sites/
    womensmedia/2012/11/09/10-steps-to-effective-listening/#6e06be143891

Exercise 3: Empathy—How to Be a "People" Person

Some people just seem to be always involved in a conflict. In many cases, it's because they don't listen or try to see things from another's perspective. Being more of a people person can be learned, and skills can be honed. Being a leader per se, or just leading yourself, often requires you to work with others as a teacher or mentor. What can you do to be more effective? Four teaching strategies are listed. [44]

- Lead by example—If you are empathic, others will likely follow your lead. How can you be a better mentor?
- Create an empathic environment—What can you do to promote compassion in the office and at home?
- Develop positive communication strategies—Create new office/personal norms that promote diversity and listening.
- Identify shared values—Complete the values exercise and have the group discuss individual and corporate values.

Take note of changes that occur in your office or home environment and check in with your direct reports, peers, customers, and supervisors to evaluate ongoing progress.

---

44 Catapano, J., No date. Teaching strategies: the importance of empathy. *TeachHub.com.*

Social Responsibility

"Stakeholders want companies to make a profit, but not at the expense of their staff and the wider community." ~ Brian Gosschalk[45]

Definition: Social responsibility is an individual's willingness to contribute to the welfare of others. This can be very broad (society in general) or more narrowly focused, such as for community groups, colleagues, and family. Social responsibility is about having a social conscience and acting responsibly.

Highs—Individuals who are highly socially responsible care about others collectively and tend to be collaborative and cooperative. They uphold social rules and norms and are seen as team players.

Lows—Individuals not high in social responsibility are more individualistic than collectivist. They tend to act or work alone and are more competitive as opposed to collaborative. Such individuals might appear withdrawn and antisocial, and they might be cut off from social activities.

You likely have heard of social responsibility in terms of CSR, which stands for Corporate Social Responsibility. The idea is the same whereby a company or corporation gives back to the community within which it operates by funding public goods, supporting local charities, and sponsoring local events. Acting this way also encompasses concern for the environment in addition to being considerate of the well-being of staff and customers.

---

45 CSR Company International., 2014. Memorable words on CSR. Retrieved from: https://www.csr-company.com/resources-corner/words/memorable-quotes-ethics-csr-and-sustainability

Exercise 1: Social Responsibility—
It Starts with You

Karen Kleinwort at *More* provides great insight into what it means to be socially responsible.[46] While we often view social responsibility as doing more for the community by "giving back," it starts from within. An individual cannot be socially responsible without being open and honest and embracing such values with passion. Critical qualities include respect, compassion, and being inspirational. To be a more socially responsible leader, you need to:

- Have personal integrity. Do you have a personal mission and a sense of how to contribute to social wellbeing? It's important to continue to learn and seek personal development. To what degree do you live by your values? Reflect on your own personal integrity.
- Consider others' perspectives. Leading requires listening. Develop your sense of compassion and care for others. How will you widen your perspective? How will you be more empathic?
- Contribute. How do you contribute to the greater good: your family, your team, your business, your community? How could you more actively participate in social development?
- Be intellectually competent. Use your reality testing to gather information to think critically about your surroundings. How can you synthesize your knowledge and resources to build something big?
- Strive for excellence. How committed are you to success over the long term? What are you doing to strive to be your best and to inspire others? How are you leading to develop creative and innovative solutions?

---

46 Kleinwort, K., No date. Business leadership: leading with social responsibility. *More*. Retrieved from: https://www.more.com/business-leadership-leading-social-responsibility

Exercise 2: Social Responsibility—Team Building

According to Sabina Nawaz, it's good practice for group members to collectively determine what is acceptable behaviour for the group and to ensure that all members of a group know what to expect.[47] More importantly, it's critical to define mutually agreed upon consequences if things go haywire.

The following are steps to take when you are working collectively. They're often referred to as "norms" and help us to enhance team effectiveness, reduce conflict, build stronger relationships, and increase productivity.

- Examine your norms. Identify them within your group.
- Which norms are working/not working?
- List the reasons for your successful norms.
- Consider norms that are unproductive and require modification.
- Review your norms periodically and make adjustments.
- Determine how you will make the norms stick.

47 Nawaz, S., 2018. How to create executive team norms—and make them stick. *Harvard Business Review.* January 15, 2018. Retrieved from: https://hbr.org/2018/01/how-to-create-executive-team-norms-and-make-them-stick

Exercise 3: Social Responsibility—Just do it!

You likely recognize Nike's tagline, "Just do it!" As a first step, Google Nike's contribution to society to get a broad idea of how that company gives back. Next, Google your favourite companies to learn about their approaches to social responsibility. You'll find a vast array of projects and programs designed to help local and global communities, individuals, and the environment.

There's no need to reinvent the wheel. Consider how you and your group will contribute. What types of projects align with your social and corporate values? What values matter to your group? John Rampton, an entrepreneur, offers the following advice to help you be more socially conscious.[48]

1. Create a mission—Identify what will work best for your business. Focus on being authentic and transparent, minimizing harm, and contributing locally. Choose something that your team/company can support.
2. Identify attainable goals—What can you accomplish and by when? Stick to realistic targets.
3. Hire well—Be sure to hire talent that is passionate about your business, including your social goals.
4. Open your doors to ideas—Crowdsource ideas for activities you could and should support. Get the local community involved and make them aware of your mission.
5. Collaborate with others—Partner with other local businesses and neighbours.
6. Establish charity rewards—Incentives matter and bonuses can be used to inspire your employees to do more.
7. Prioritize social responsibility—Make "giving" part of your core values.

---

48 Rampton, J., 2017. 7 Ways to make your business more socially conscious. *Social Entrepreneurship*. January 27, 2017. Retrieved from: https://www.entrepreneur.com/article/288339

DECISION MAKING

Problem-Solving

Reality Testing

Impulse Control

？

BEING DECISIVE

Have you ever experienced intense emotions and at the same time had to make a decision? Emotions can influence decisions both positively and negatively and sometimes prevent decision making entirely. Furthermore, emotions entirely unrelated to a situation can influence decisions. Research shows that individuals with low emotional intelligence tend to rely on emotions to make decisions,[49] whereas those with high EI are aware of their emotions but can objectively make decisions.[50]

Decision making is highly important in the workplace, particularly because emotions might cloud judgements, resulting in problems. Consider the customer service rep who has had an argument with a spouse before work and a challenging commute given bad weather. The rep is unhappy, frustrated, and somewhat anxious. The first thing on the agenda is an unhappy long-term customer. Letting unrelated emotions get in the way could result in irrational decisions and perhaps jeopardize the relationship and future business.

Another example that clearly demonstrates this principle is "road rage." Anger and rage result in physiological changes to the body that prevent rational thought. While it's annoying and sometimes dangerous when other motorists behave erratically, it does not warrant such severe actions as fistfights and shootings!

Individuals skilled in this realm understand how to solve problems where emotions are concerned and to evaluate facts objectively. They are also in control of their emotions and do not act rashly or impulsively. On the contrary, those not skilled in

---

49 Khazan, O., 2016. The best headspace for making decisions. *The Atlantic*, Sept 19, 2016. Retrieved from: https://www.theatlantic.com/science/archive/2016/09/the-best-headspace-for-making-decisions/500423/

50 Anonymous., 2013. How Emotional Intelligence Can Improve Decision-Making. *Huffington Post*, November 22, 2013. Retrieved from: https://www.huffpost.com/entry/emotional-intelligence-decision-making_n_4310192

this realm will allow emotions to rule their decisions, they will likely have difficulty solving problems in emotional situations, they don't see all the facts, and they are often impulsive.

"It does not take much strength to do things, but it requires a great deal of strength to decide what to do." ~ Elbert Hubbard[51]

---

51 Optimize., 2020. Retrieved from: https://www.optimize.me/quotes/
elbert-hubbard/20739-it-does-not-take-much-strength-to-do-thi/

Problem-Solving

"When dealing with people, remember you are not dealing with creatures of logic, but with creatures of emotion." ~ Dale Carnegie[52]

Definition: Problem-solving is defined as the ability to make objective decisions where emotions are concerned. Our ability to solve problems can be tempered by our emotions, resulting in unwanted outcomes.

Highs—Individuals skilled in problem-solving can focus on the issue and understand how emotions can be used appropriately to arrive at a decision. They're able to select an appropriate course of action objectively.

Lows—People who are not strong problem-solvers are often overcome by emotions; they're less focused and unable to arrive at a decision. They also might appear anxious and distraught.

Problem-solving is very important to leadership and is one of the factors that can derail a leader. Without the ability to solve problems, leaders are less likely able to manage their staff, make decisions, or accomplish objectives.

---

52 Forbes., 2011. Forbes Quotes: Thoughts on the Business of Life. Retrieved from: https://www.forbes.com/quotes/2024/

Exercise 1: Problem-Solving—
A Step-Wise Process

Lynn Sylva proposes a methodical approach to thinking clearly during decision making, particularly where emotions are concerned.[53] She recommends the following tips:

- Rely on a healthy attitude—Be mindful of your own emotions and work to stay calm, open-minded, and positive. Do not let emotions cloud the facts.
- Use impulse control—Be mindful of when to jump in with ideas and when to let others speak.
- Fully articulate the problem—Defining a problem is the first step to solving it. This will require you to evaluate facts and test assumptions. Do you have all the information necessary? How can you get the information you need?
- Determine the source of the problem—Play the Devil's advocate to ensure you can see the problem from all perspectives.
- Be open to all possible solutions—Use your co-workers to brainstorm potential solutions.
- Do not procrastinate if a decision is required—Avoiding a problem or waiting for it to go away might make it worse.
- Delegate where possible—Define who will be responsible for the solution/resolution.
- Establish clear outcomes—Set standards and a deadline for the solution to be implemented.
- Move forward—Take action!
- Evaluate the process—If the problem isn't solved, redefine it and repeat the process.

---

53 Sylva, L., No date. The Simplest Ways to Improve Your Problem Solving Skills. *Lifehack*. Retrieved from: https://www.lifehack.org/articles/productivity/the-simplest-ways-improve-your-problem-solving-skills.html

Exercise 2: Problem-Solving—Hurson's Model[54]

This model, also known as ThinkX, was developed by Tim Hurson. It's a simple but deceptively effective framework based on six steps that helps to solve problems creatively. Stretch yourself (or the group) as you go through the following steps. Be sure to consider all the questions.

Step 1: Articulate the problem

- What are the likely effects or outcomes?
- What information is available?
- What information is needed?
- Who is involved?
- Envision the future.

Step 2: Define success

- What steps are required for success?
- What are the criteria for success?

Step 3: Express questions that require answers

- What are the essential questions that must be answered to achieve the vision?
- Prioritize questions to find the "right" questions.

Step 4: Generate answers

- Brainstorm as many ideas as possible to answer the questions you developed in Step 3.
- Start identifying the best ideas from which to choose.

Step 5: Forge the solution

- Select the best ideas from Step 4.
- Compare ideas according to success criteria from Step 2.
- Consider further development of ideas that meet the criteria.

---

54 Mulder, P., No date. Productive Thinking Model (PTM). Toolshero. Retrieved from: https://www.toolshero.com/problem-solving/productive-thinking-model/

Step 6: Align resources

- Determine the actions and resources necessary to implement the best idea.
- Identify personnel required and define responsibilities.

Exercise 3: Problem-Solving— The Deming Wheel[55]

The Deming Wheel, developed by W. Edwards Deming, is also known as PDCA (plan-do-check-act). The model outlines an iterative process that helps take emotion out of decision making and helps individuals move through a cycle of continuous improvement.

Plan: Articulate the problem or opportunity and analyze it for potential problems. Develop several testable hypotheses and select the best one to test.

Do: Test for a solution on a small scale and measure the results. This might be done using a pilot project.

Check: Examine the results and evaluate them for effectiveness and other important criteria. Determine whether the hypothesis is supported.

Act: If the solution was successful, implement it. If the solution wasn't successful, repeat the process and make corrections and adjustments.

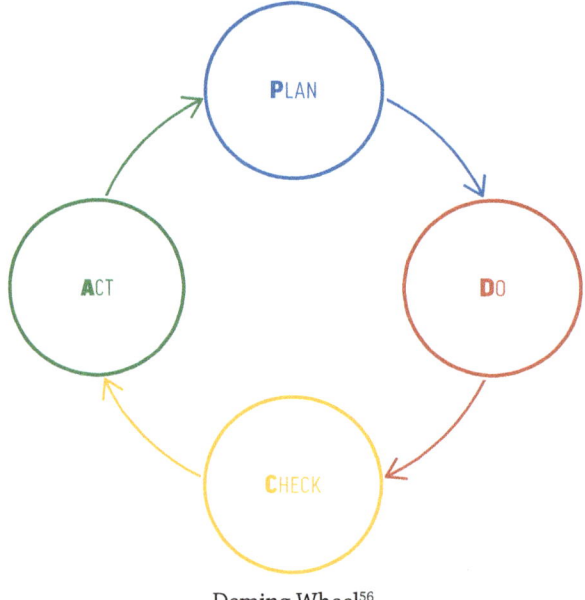

Deming Wheel[56]

55 MindTools Content Team. No date. Plan-Do-Check-Act (PDCA). *MindTools*. Retrieved from: https://www.mindtools.com/pages/article/newPPM_89.htm

56 Bulsuk, K. No date. Retrieved from: http://www.bulsuk.com

Reality Testing

"Your excuses might be legit, but they won't improve your life." ~ Grant Cardone[57]

Definition: Reality testing is the ability to see situations as they really are; to observe the facts objectively and impartially.

Highs—People skilled at reality testing gather all the facts, see a situation objectively, set realistic goals, and make rational decisions. These individuals are seen as grounded and able to separate emotions from facts.

Lows—Individuals not skilled in reality testing will often make unrealistic promises, are missing information, and do not consider all the facts. They allow emotions to cloud judgements, and they have difficulty separating emotion from fact.

According to Sigmund Freud, reality testing is the ability to recognize the difference between what's happening externally and how you perceive things internally. Another way to put it would be to see things as they really are, and not what you are hoping or wishing they would be.

57 Cardone, G., 2015. Excuses Will Not Create Your Super Life. Medium. Retrieved from: https://medium.com/@grantcardone/excuses-will-not-create-your-super-life-b120469cdef

Exercise 1: Reality Testing – Errors in Thought

There are many reasons for not seeing things objectively.[58] Do you or someone you know make some of the following errors in thought?

- All or nothing—polarized or "black-and-white" thinking. Things are all good or all bad; there is no middle ground
- Overgeneralization—taking one problem and generalizing to be the rule
- Mental filters—seeing only the negative or positive (similar to overgeneralization)
- Positive disqualification—recognizing positive experiences but rejecting them
- Mind reading—relying on assumptions as facts; inaccurate beliefs
- Fortune telling—false or biased predictions about the future
- Catastrophizing—exaggerating the importance or meaning of something
- Emotional reasoning—using emotions as facts or truths
- Labelling/mislabelling—applying highly emotionally-loaded language and acting accordingly

The solution is to reframe or redirect your thoughts.

- Think of an example of a situation in which you or someone made a mental error and identify it.
- Consider different perspectives. How else could you state the problem?
- Define more realistic thoughts.
- Identify a more appropriate solution or outcome.

Try it with one of the errors above.

---

58 Ackerman, Courtney. 2017. Cognitive Distortions: When Your Brain Lies to You.
    Positive Psychology Program. Retrieved from: https://positivepsychologyprogram.com/
    cognitive-distortions/

Exercise 2: Reality Testing—
Getting the best of you?

It's great to be prepared, but sometimes we let negative thinking about worst-case scenarios get out of hand. We act according to our thoughts and beliefs, which can be incorrect. Reality testing is highly important to judge situations appropriately and act and react appropriately. Joshua Miles, an integrative psychotherapist, suggests answering the following questions to help improve reality testing.[59]

- What are the facts?
- What are the possible perspectives?
- What are you feeling?
- What are you thinking?
- What are some external perspectives?
- Who could you ask?
- When will you ask?
- What will you do with the information?

Take time to make decisions and separate emotions from facts.

---

59 Miles, J., 2015. What is reality testing and why is it important? *Counselling Directory*. October *26, 2015*. Retrieved from: https://www.counselling-directory.org.uk/counsellor-articles/ what-is-reality-testing-why-is-it-important

Exercise 3: Reality Testing—Anger

Dr. Harry Mills talks specifically about the intensity of anger as an emotion.[60] Angry people are unable to make clear decisions: they are overcome with rage, often succumb to black and white thinking, and act highly inappropriately, often losing control. To gain control, practise being mindful.

Control your thoughts

- What specifically makes you angry? What is the meaning?
- How can you improve the situation?
- Focus on relaxing. Take time to calm down.

Test reality

- Who are you blaming?
- Is this realistic?
- What are your assumptions?
- How can you give them up?
- How will you collect more information?

Black and white thinking

- Pay attention to your language. Is it polarized?
- Pause and consider the nuances of a situation.
- Talk with others to gain a new perspective.
- Consider alternative possibilities.

The benefit of the doubt

- Think of alternative scenarios to a situation.
- Give the subject of your anger the benefit of the doubt.

---

60 Mills, H., No date. Reality testing and anger management. *MentalHelp.net*. Retrieved from: https://www.mentalhelp.net/articles/reality-testing-and-anger-management/

Impulse control

"I cannot trust a man to control others if he cannot control himself." ~ Robert E. Lee[61]

Definition: Impulse control is the ability to control urges and delay gratification, which can prevent rash decisions. It's important to be able to manage emotions to build trust by acting thoughtfully.

Highs—People who are highly skilled in this regard are very much in control of their emotions and actions. They can resist the urge to speak or act; they behave deliberately in a composed and calculative manner.

Lows—Impulsive people often speak and act before thinking of the consequences; they are often impatient and overactive. Such individuals often are unpredictable and spontaneous, and they might regret the consequences of their actions.

Impulsive people tend to act first and think later. This can result in poor judgement and bad decisions, and eventually erode trust. While being decisive can be a boon in certain situations, there can be a fine line between thinking a situation through and acting hastily without sufficient preparation.

---

61 BrainyQuote., No date. Retrieved from: https://www.brainyquote.com/quotes/ robert_e_lee_383501

Exercise 1: Impulse Control—
Look Before You Leap

Forbes Coaches Council recognized impulse control, or the lack thereof, to be critically important for leaders.[62] The top eight of 17 strategies to manage impulsive behaviour are listed here.

- Press pause—Take time to think and then act.
- Talk through the process—Consider all the angles then talk to others to gain a greater perspective.
- Make a list of the facts—Be clear about what is at stake and make sure you have all the information necessary to make a decision.
- Rely on a colleague—Use someone you trust as a sounding board with whom to share ideas and thoughts before acting.
- Listen—Using active listening can be revealing.
- Be patient—"Patience is a virtue" means that you have the strength and ability to wait without being frustrated and angry.
- Slow down—Take time to think and then react.
- Get the big picture—While the facts are in the details, it's useful to see the whole picture.

Do you have *all* types of information necessary to make a decision?

---

62 Forbes Coaches Council., 2017. Look before you leap. *Forbes.com*. October 18, 2017. Retrieved from: https://www.forbes.com/sites/forbescoachescouncil/2017/10/18/look-before-you-leap-17-ways-to-slow-down-impulsive-decisions/#6bfc170b4440

Exercise 2: Impulse Control—Be Ready

If you are impulsive, how do you manage the impulses? The first step is to be prepared, according to Thomas Plante.[63]

1. Know your risks—If you know yourself and understand what makes you impulsive, you can develop strategies before you need them. Make a list of your risks.

2. Plan for your risks—Once you understand what triggers you, change your environment. How can you modify your environment?

3. Use time—Count to 10 to buy some time and delay action.

4. Be mindful—Pay attention to what you are feeling, the emotions that arise, and your behaviours. How will you remain mindful of your feelings?

5. Get feedback—Ask a colleague or someone you trust to provide corrections or reminders when necessary. Who will you ask?

6. Practise—Change is not easy and will occur only when you make new behaviours a habit. What do you need to motivate you?

---

63 Plante, T., 2010. Six principles to best manage impulses to maximize life satisfaction and success. *Psychology Today,* May 16, 2010. Retrieved from: https://www.psychologytoday.com/us/blog/do-the-right-thing/201005/six-principles-best-manage-impulses-maximize-life-satisfaction-and-success

Exercise 3: Impulse Control—Self-Control

Staying in control as a leader requires judicious thinking and the ability to manage yourself. To improve your self-control, consider the following options suggested by Bruna Martinuzzi,[64] a trainer at American Express Company.

- Apply logic to your worries—Using reality testing to be objective can help you to gain perspective.
- Stay clear of office drama—While it's good to be in the trenches, you do need a certain amount of distance to stay in control.
- Manage your technology—Use auto settings to delay sending an email or responding to messages. Buy some time to be thoughtful.
- Turn off technology—Put the phone away so as not to react to alerts that trigger emotions.
- Control your personal communications—Be aware of your language and body language when you act and react to people and situations. Modify your responses to better manage yourself when you're in a critical situation.
- Buy time—Taking time for yourself to reflect and think can help you to reset and calm yourself to prevent dragging emotions from one situation to the next.
- Be mindful of your triggers—Understand what sets you off and be prepared. Being mindful of your own impulsive actions is a first step to making changes.

---

64 Martinuzzi, B., 2016. 7 Tips to help improve your emotional self-control and leadership. *American Express Company*. May 30, 2016. Retrieved from: https://www.americanexpress.com/en-us/business/trends-and-insights/articles/emotional-self-control-and-leadership/

STRESS MANAGEMENT

Flexibility

Stress Tolerance

Optimism

STRESSED OUT

Stress is a growing concern in society, as evidenced by the increasing number of individuals requiring medical leave for conditions brought on by stress.[65,66] And there are predictions of future increases.[67] Stress is caused by everything from greater demands at work, to running kids to an increasing number of extracurricular activities, and everything in between. Many studies have evaluated the effects of stress on people in the workplace, on students and academic achievement, and on leadership.[68] Other studies have examined the negative effect stress has on health.[69]

While technology was supposed to make lives easier, it seems that advances in computing and telecommunications are creeping into our private lives, making it more difficult to relax and separate work from home. Stress starts early as well. This seems to be true for students in their teenage years[70] and is the case for students pursuing higher education.[71]

65 Staff., 2018. Canadian employers expect rise in medical leaves due to mental health: survey. Benefits Canada, March 22. Retrieved from: https://www.benefitscanada.com/news/canadian-employers-expect-increase-in-employee-medical-leaves-survey-112373

66 Staff., 2018. "Epidemic of stress" blamed for 3,750 teachers on long-term sick leave. The Guardian, January 11, 2018. Retrieved from: https://www.theguardian.com/education/2018/jan/11/epidemic-of-stress-blamed-for-3750-teachers-on-longterm-sick-leave

67 Shea, M., 2017. American stress is on the rise. New York Post, February 16, 2017. Retrieved from: https://nypost.com/2017/02/16/american-stress-is-on-the-rise/

68 Smith, M. & Cooper, C., 1994. Leadership and stress. Leadership & Organization Development Journal, 15(2), pp.3-7.

69 Herr, R.M., Barrech, A., Riedel, N., Gündel, H., Angerer, P. & Li, J., 2018. Long-term effectiveness of stress management at work: Effects of the changes in perceived stress reactivity on mental health and sleep problems seven years later. *International journal of environmental research and public health*, 15(2), p.255.

70 Mazziotta, J., 2018. Teen stress is on the rise: why it's a major problem, and how you can help. People Magazine, May 14, 2018. Retrieved from: https://people.com/health/teen-stress-rising-what-to-do/

71 Racco, M., 2018. This is the state of stress in 2018. Global News, April 16, 2018. Retrieved from: https://globalnews.ca/news/4138006/stress-causes-today/

Those who can manage stress are generally flexible, have many diverse coping mechanisms, and are optimistic about the future, particularly during difficult or challenging times. Alternatively, those less able to handle stress react negatively to change, don't know how to cope, and are somewhat pessimistic.

Flexibility

Definition: Flexibility is the willingness and ability to adapt to change and to respond to new information and situations. It's important because change is common and rigidity can lead to missed opportunities, a lack of innovation, and challenging relationships.

Highs—Highly flexible people are willing to change their minds when presented with new information, to adapt to changing situations, and to be enabling and accommodating when appropriate.

Lows—People who aren't very flexible see only one way to accomplish tasks, they are unwilling to consider new ideas and information, they are less accommodating, and they rarely stray from structured processes and procedures.

How can you become more flexible? How could you help others expand their willingness to accept new ideas, challenges, processes, and procedures?

"The measure of intelligence is the ability to change." ~ Albert Einstein[72]

---

72 Goodreads., No date. Retrieved from: https://www.goodreads.com/quotes/85475-the-measure-of-intelligence-is-the-ability-to-change

Exercise 1: Flexibility—Give a Little

For each of the following statements, give an example of an appropriate flexible response and the positive outcomes that could occur:

- allowing some employees to work from home,
- staggering work shifts to accommodate different employees' needs,
- delegating important tasks,
- accommodating a customer who requires special assistance after hours,
- hearing that your company will change its communication software,
- learning you have to work overtime,
- hearing constructive criticism regarding your performance,
- covering for an employee while they are on parental leave,
- using new social media outlets for some marketing,
- dropping what you are doing to handle a crisis,
- adopting suggestions to do things a different way,
- considering customer suggestions regarding your product or service.

Use your own examples. List five things you do for which increased flexibility might change the outcome.

Be sure to reflect on the benefits.

For more on flexibility, see American Recruiters.[73]

---

73 Doyle, A., 2017. Workplace flexibility, definition, skills, and examples. *American Recruiters*, February 27, 2017. Retrieved from: https://www.americanrecruiters.com/2017/02/27/workplace-flexibility-definition-skills-examples/

Exercise 2: Flexibility—Change Is the Only Constant

Being flexible is about managing change, which can be difficult for some. Change often elicits negative emotions such as fear, anxiety, and apprehension. At the same time, being too flexible could come across as being wishy-washy. To be able to handle change appropriately, we often need to be sufficiently flexible to change beliefs, attitudes, and thoughts. What follows is a change in behaviour.

Consider a personal or workplace situation in which you are being asked to change. How would you respond to the following points?

Overcome irrational fears—*change your beliefs*

- List your emotions associated with the situation.
- Do they tend to be more positive or negative?
- What do you believe will happen?
- Is this realistic?

Set new goals—*get focused*

- What is your goal for getting through the process?
- What beliefs do you need to change to overcome your emotions?

Anticipate change—*reduce the uncertainty*

- What do you expect will happen?
- How does that make you feel?
- What steps could you take to be prepared?

Embrace the process—*replace ambiguity with information*

- Make a list of the information you have and the information you don't have.
- How will you collect the necessary information?
- When will you start?

Stretch yourself—*innovate ahead of the curve*

- What new things can you do to keep learning?
- How will you embrace learning?
- What are your beliefs about learning?

Exercise 3: Flexibility—A Rock and a Hard Place

Leaders are often put in challenging situations because being flexible is sometimes not possible. When it's not appropriate to bend rules, make concessions, or accommodate a request, a leader can be seen as being inflexible. However, being flexible in some situations can lead to better morale and higher performance. Use the following exercise to define what flexibility means to you and what it looks like. You could use this approach with a team to enhance communication and to learn what your group values most.

1. Consider a time when you were asked to make a concession and did.
   - What did you do?
   - What were your reasons?
   - What criteria did you use?
   - What were the outcomes?
   - What would you do differently?

2. Think of another example when you were asked but decided not to make concessions.
   - What did you do?
   - What were your reasons?
   - What criteria did you use?
   - What were the outcomes?
   - What would you do differently?

Be sure to work with your coach or debrief this exercise as a team.

- What went wrong?
- What worked?
- What were the advantages and disadvantages of being flexible?
- How were you perceived?
- What emotions did you experience?

It's important to consider how you balance flexibility with problem-solving, independence, and impulse control.

For more reading on the importance of flexibility for leadership, see the article by Jeanette Landin.[74]

---

74 Landin, J., 2017. Keys to flexible leadership. *Strategic Finance*, October 1, 2017. Retrieved from: https://sfmagazine.com/post-entry/october-2017-keys-to-flexible-leadership/

Stress Tolerance

Definition: Stress tolerance is your general ability to deal with challenging situations in a healthy way.

Highs—Individuals who can handle stress are generally calm under pressure, can handle their emotions, have a variety of coping mechanisms, and are resilient.

Lows—Individuals who demonstrate lower stress tolerance have few coping mechanisms, are not in control of their emotions, are not as focused, and can be somewhat anxious. In severe cases, people might require medical attention.

Stress tolerance is key to leadership. Consider leaders you've had in the past. What was it like working for a leader who could handle stress as opposed to one who couldn't? It's often the case that stressed leaders make for stressed followers.

"It's not the load that breaks you down. It's the way you carry it." ~ Lena Horne[75]

---

75 Quotefancy., No date. Retrieved from: https://quotefancy.com/quote/1243981/
    Lena-Horne-It-s-not-the-load-that-breaks-you-down-it-s-the-way-you-carry-it-Carry-it-by

Exercise 1: Stress Tolerance—Get Organized

According to Kenneth Mattos, leaders who are stressed fail to practice empathy and thus create a downward spiral of emotions, which leads to frustration for all parties.[76]

To help handle the stress, he suggests several options. Consider the following suggestions by identifying what *you* could do and how *you* will benefit.

1. Make a priority list. It's not enough to make a "to-do" list; it's important to go one step further by prioritizing things on the list. Then focus on getting the top priority items finished.
2. Add personal priorities to your list. To achieve a healthy work/life balance, you need to consider all priorities.
3. Share your list with your boss/peers/direct reports. The more they know what you're balancing, the more understanding there will be for your situation. Sharing helps to build trust and improve authenticity.
4. Share responsibility. It's tough to go it alone. Delegate and work together to get important tasks done. How will you delegate? What will you delegate? To whom?
5. Set and articulate boundaries. Are you the kind of person who works long after quitting time? Perhaps it's time to turn off your work phone and email alerts. Make it known that you are not available, and stick to your guns.

After two weeks, review your list and reflect on what has changed.

What emotions are you feeling?

How can you continue to mitigate stress by tweaking your list?

---

76 Mattos, K., Training leaders to manage stress and improve organizational performance. Training industry, May 8, 2017. Retrieved from: https://trainingindustry.com/articles/leadership/training-leaders-to-manage-stress-and-improve-organizational-performance/

Exercise 2: Stress Tolerance—The Mayo Way

You might not be able to run the Boston Marathon, nor want to, but any exercise, in any form, according to the Mayo Clinic, can help to relieve stress.[77] There are three reasons why exercise can help: it increases endorphins, which helps you to feel better; it is akin to meditation in that you forget the tensions at the office or at home; and it can enhance your mood through relaxation and better sleep.

Take the following steps to reduce stress through exercise:

- Consult with your doctor first to ensure you are fit. Your choice of activity will likely depend on your level of fitness and your interest.
- Start slowly. Don't try to run a marathon on your first day. A five-minute walk is a good first step. Build up gradually to avoid overdoing it and sustaining an injury.
- Do what you love and what interests you. If you're not interested in aerobics or Zumba, it's not likely that you'll follow through with the exercise. Be sure to do something you enjoy!
- Schedule it and make it a priority. Add it to your list and make it one of the most important events in your week. We often hear that there's no time for exercise; however, if we don't take care of ourselves, there will be no work either!
- Make it a habit. Work with a friend, diversify to keep it exciting, and do it in short stints. Don't succumb to errors in thinking that sound like this: I can't make it for an hour, so I might as well not bother.

Explain how you will commit to getting more exercise.

---

77 Mayo Clinic., No date. Healthy lifestyle: stress management. Retrieved from: https://www. mayoclinic.org/healthy-lifestyle/stress-management/in-depth/exercise-and-stress/art-20044469

Exercise 3: Stress Tolerance—Meditation

Meditation has long been associated with stress management and healthy living. There is a plethora of research, books, classes, and apps to help you start your practice. Matthew Thorpe reports on scientifically-evaluated benefits of meditation, which are many and include reduced stress, reduced anxiety, greater emotional health and self- awareness, a heightened ability to focus, and better memory, just to name a few.[78]

If you want to try meditating on your own, there are several approaches. The most basic approach includes the following steps suggested by Inner IDEA:[79]

1. Make yourself comfortable by sitting on a chair or mat or by lying down.
2. Make no effort to control your breath; simply breathe naturally.
3. Close your eyes.
4. Focus your attention on the breath and on how the body moves with each inhalation and exhalation.
5. Notice the movement of your body as you breathe.
6. Observe your chest, shoulders, rib cage, and belly. Simply focus your attention on your breath without controlling its pace or intensity. If your mind wanders, return your focus back to your breath.

Begin your practice with a few minutes a day. It might even be two minutes at your desk. You'll notice how tense you are and should immediately feel the benefits of slowing down. Build your practice and take note of what is working and make changes accordingly. More reading on meditation can be found at VeryWellMind.[80]

---

78 Thorpe, M., 2017. 12 Science-based benefits of meditation. Healthline.com. July 5, 2017. Retrieved from: https://www.healthline.com/nutrition/12-benefits-of-meditation

79 Inner IDEA., 2018. Meditation 101: techniques, benefits, and a beginner's how-to. GAIAM. Retrieved from: https://www.gaiam.com/blogs/discover/meditation-101-techniques-benefits-and-a-beginner-s-how-to

80 Scott, E., 2018. Practice basic mediation for stress management. Verywellmind.com. May 18, 2018. Retrieved from: https://www.verywellmind.com/practice-basic-meditation-for-stress-management-3144789

Optimism

Optimism is important in the workplace to inspire those around us to rise to challenges and work through difficulties. Research shows that optimistic salespeople make significantly more sales.[81]

Definition: Optimism is hopefulness and confidence about the future. It's about being resilient and having a positive attitude, particularly when facing challenges.

Highs—Optimistic people are generally very positive and pleasant to be around. They see the glass as half full and are hopeful about the future concerning themselves and most everything else.

Lows—People who are not optimistic are very negative and tend to be pessimistic about the future. They are less resilient in the face of setbacks and don't expect good things for themselves or future outcomes.

If you're not the type of person who was born optimistic, it's not too late! You can practise being optimistic by looking to the future and changing your focus. The following three exercises can help to change your view of the world with a little bit of practice.

"Don't cry because it's over, smile because it happened." ~ Ludwig Jacobowski[82]

---

81 Stajkovic, A. D., Lee, D., Greenwald, J. M., & Raffiee, J., 2015. The role of trait core confidence higher-order construct in self-regulation of performance and attitudes: Evidence from four studies. Organizational Behavior and Human Decision Processes, 128, 29–48.

82 Quote Investigator., 2016. Don't Cry Because It's Over; Smile Because It Happened. Retrieved from: https://quoteinvestigator.com/2016/07/25/smile/

Exercise 1: Optimism—Change Your Focus

While you might not be the most optimistic person, it's not impossible to change. It requires attention and practice. The following steps can help you identify when you are pessimistic and what prevents you from being more optimistic. Take a few minutes to consider the following suggestions:

- Avoid negative environments—Make a list of negative environments that might be depressing your thoughts and actions. What can you do to avoid them?
- Focus outside of yourself—What are the positive influences in your life? Consider all external factors, including work, family, friends, travel, etc.
- Nurture a culture of optimism through self-talk and positive behaviour— Reflect on the negative words you tend to use. Replace each with a positive word.
- Celebrate your strengths—List your strengths, best features, and that for which you are grateful.

Once you have considered the suggestions above, think about …

- What factors are most important for you.
- What you will do to make changes.
- How you will hold yourself accountable.

Ignore/accept what you cannot change. Reflect on what is beyond your control. What is preventing you from letting go?

Be sure to check in with yourself in two-four weeks to evaluate your changes and reflect on the benefits.

Exercise 2: Optimism—Reframe Your Thinking

Megan Wicklendt reports on the scientific relationship between optimism and a positive attitude, and happiness and success.[83] Think about the people you spend time with and how their penchant for either optimism or pessimism affects you. You might notice that the more optimistic the person, the more uplifting and fun they are. The alternative is also true—chronic pessimists can drain your energy.

Three suggestions from Ms. Wicklendt's article are suggested here:

- Keep a gratitude journal. Being thankful for what we have and regularly acknowledging our fortunes can help us focus on what's good about our lives. Reflect daily on everything for which you are grateful. This exercise will require you to focus less on negative things in your environment and create a habit of looking at the positive.
- Reframing your thinking is often used by executive coaches to help their clients see different perspectives. For example, a failure might become a learning experience, which is positive because you have more information and experience moving forward.
- Change your vocabulary. Take note of how many negative words you use and start to replace them with positive words. If you describe your life as "boring, busy, mundane, chaotic," that's how you'll perceive it, and you will feel the effects in your body and mind. If you use the words "simple, involved, familiar or lively," you'll see your life in a whole different light and find more enjoyment in the way you chose to shape your life.

---

83 Wycklendt, M., 2014. 10 Simple habits to grow a positive attitude. *Fulfillment Daily*, August 4, 2014. Retrieved from: http://www.fulfillmentdaily.com/10-habits-to-grow-a-positive-attitude/

Exercise 3: Optimism—Mental Subtraction

This exercise was derived from a study at the University of California, Berkeley that looks at the relationship between behaviour and the ability to be happy and healthy.[84] To practise optimism, consider what would happen *without* some of the good things in your life. The steps as listed on the *Greater Good in Action* website[85] are as follows:

1. Take a moment to think about a positive event in your life, such as an educational or career achievement, the birth of a child, or a special trip you took.
2. Think back to the time of this event and the circumstances that made it possible.
3. Consider how this event might never have happened—for example, if you hadn't learned about a certain job opening at the right moment.
4. Write down all of the possible events and decisions—large and small—that could have gone differently and prevented this event from occurring.
5. Imagine what your life would be like now if you hadn't enjoyed this positive event and all the fruits that flowed from it.
6. Shift your focus to remind yourself that this event actually did happen and reflect upon the benefits it has brought you.

Now that you have considered how things might have turned out differently, appreciate that these benefits were not inevitable in your life. Allow yourself to feel grateful that things happened as they did.

---

84 Koo, M., Algoe, S. B., Wilson, T. D., & Gilbert, D. T., 2008. It's a wonderful life: mentally subtracting positive events improves people's affective states, contrary to their affective forecasts. *Journal of Personality and Social Psychology*, 95(5), 1217.

85 No Author., No date. Mental subtraction of positive events. Greater Good in Action. Retrieved from: https://ggia.berkeley.edu/practice/

FINAL THOUGHTS

You should now be well on your way to enhancing the emotional skills that are important to you. While it might be difficult or even uncomfortable at first, it is a sign that you are learning and growing. Continued mindfulness and practise will help you to hone your skills such that they become natural.

Over time, you should start to notice changes in how you see and react to the world around you. You might be more aware of your emotions and how you appropriately express yourself. Perhaps you take more time to think before reacting and can better manage your stress. You might also start to notice that others are drawn to you and see you with greater respect in light of your heightened skills and awareness.

Continuing to be mindful of your emotions and how you govern yourself will lead to enhanced well-being both personally and professionally. If you are leading others, they will notice your ability to be authentic, innovative and insightful, and to help others to be their best. Such skills are more difficult to master, but will have lasting and significant effects. Persistence will ensure that you continue to develop emotional skills throughout your life resulting in a greater sense of wellbeing.

www.ingramcontent.com/pod-product-compliance
Lightning Source LLC
Chambersburg PA
CBHW041130280526
45792CB00013B/2373